THE SECRET PLACE

THE SECRET PLACE

ALIGNING WITH GOD
FOR POWER AND RESTORATION

CECIL E.
BRIDGEFORTH

CONCISE
PUBLISHING HOUSE

The Secret Place: *Aligning with God for Power and Restoration*

©2026 by Cecil E. Bridgeforth. All rights reserved.

ISBN: 979-8-9951378-0-1

No part of this publication may be reproduced, distributed, or transmitted in any form or by any means, including photocopying, recording, or other electronic or mechanical methods, without the prior written permission of the publisher, except in the case of brief quotations embodied in critical reviews and certain other noncommercial uses permitted by copyright law. For permission requests, write to the publisher, addressed "Attention: Permissions Coordinator," at the address below:

Concise Publishing House
120 Preston Executive Drive, Suite 229
Cary, NC 27513
www.ConcisePublishing.us

Scripture taken from the New King James Version®. Copyright © 1982 by Thomas Nelson. Used by permission. All rights reserved. Scripture quotations marked (KJV) are from the King James Version of the Bible.

In Loving Memory of
Rev. Dr. Cecil Bridgeforth
A Man of Faith, Power, and Prayer

Contents

OPENING PRAYER

Father, we enter Your presence with reverence and expectation. Prayer is not ritual. It is relationship. As we begin this journey, align our hearts with Your will and silence every distraction that competes for our attention. Open our understanding. Correct our thinking. Strengthen our discipline.

Teach us to seek You intentionally and consistently. Remove complacency. Ignite spiritual hunger within us. Establish in us a deeper desire for communion with You. Let this book produce obedience, not information.

Position us in the Secret Place. Train our hearts to respond to Your voice. Guard us from pride and self-reliance. Let alignment produce manifestation and obedience release promise.

As we read, instruct us. As we learn, transform us. As we pray, respond according to Your will and Your Word. We commit ourselves to disciplined pursuit of Your presence. In Jesus' name, Amen.

INTRODUCTION

In a world filled with noise, distractions, and constant movement, there remains a sacred invitation, a call to step away from the crowd and enter *The Secret Place*. It is there, in the quiet chambers of communion with God, that strength is renewed, purpose is revealed, and hearts are transformed.

Prayer is more than words spoken into the air. It is the language of intimacy between the Creator and His creation. In *The Secret Place*, we do not perform. We abide. We do not strive to be heard. We listen. It is where burdens are lifted, battles are won, and the power of the Holy Spirit is released into our lives.

Every believer must discover the treasure hidden in this divine exchange. *The Secret Place* is not reserved for the few. It is entered by those who seek Him earnestly. The deeper you go in prayer, the greater the revelation, strength, and authority you carry in your walk with God.

As you journey through this reading, let your spirit be stirred to dwell in the presence of the Almighty, not occasionally, but continually. For in

The Secret Place, the ordinary becomes extraordinary, and the weak become strong through the power of prayer.

Prayer is not mastered through explanation alone. It is cultivated through participation. As you read, do not remain an observer. Engage. Align. Respond. The Secret Place is not discovered through information, but through intentional pursuit.

CHAPTER 1
The Power of Prayer

Then you will call upon Me and go and pray to Me, and I will listen to you. And you will seek Me and find Me, when you search for Me with all your heart.
Jeremiah 29:12–13 NKJV

What Is Prayer?

Prayer is the sacred communication between humanity and God. It is the dialogue of the soul with its Creator, where words, worship, and even silence become the language of the heart. It is a divine exchange where we pour out our hearts and receive His presence, power, and peace.

To pray is to invite Heaven into the affairs of earth. It aligns our will with God's will and draws strength from His wisdom. Prayer is not one-sided; God listens, and He speaks. In stillness, His whisper brings clarity, conviction, and comfort.

The Purpose of Prayer

Prayer was designed to produce transformation, not performance. Through prayer we:

- Connect with God personally
- Communicate our needs and gratitude
- Consecrate ourselves to His purpose
- Conquer spiritual battles that cannot be won in the flesh

The purpose of prayer is not to change God's mind, but to align ours with His. When you truly pray, panic gives way to peace and earthly perspective shifts toward divine understanding.

Prayer as Relationship

Prayer reveals the depth of your relationship with God. Just as intimacy requires communication, spiritual intimacy requires prayer. In the Secret Place, you know God not only as Lord, but as Father. You experience His heart, not just His hand.

Jesus modeled this continually. Before miracles, before decisions, before the cross; He prayed. If the Son of God maintained constant communion with the Father, how much more must we?

Dimensions of Prayer

There are many ways to express prayer, each unlocking a different dimension of relationship with God:

- Adoration - honoring God for who He is
- Confession - aligning the heart through repentance
- Thanksgiving - expressing gratitude
- Supplication - presenting requests in faith
- Intercession - standing in the gap for others

Each of these expressions draws us deeper into the presence of God. When combined, they form a full picture of what it means to walk in spiritual communion.

The Power Behind Prayer

The true power of prayer does not come from the eloquence of our words, but from the sincerity of our hearts. God responds to faith, not formulas. He listens to the brokenhearted, the humble, and the persistent.

Prayer carries creative power. It builds, restores, and transforms. When we pray according to God's Word, we release His will into the atmosphere. Prayer can shift nations, heal bodies, restore families, and ignite revival

Prayer is the divine lifeline between heaven and earth. It is the believer's greatest weapon, the key that unlocks God's power, and the bridge that connects human weakness to divine strength.

The enemy fears a praying believer because prayer activates heaven's authority on earth. It silences doubt, defeats fear, and releases supernatural strategy. Prayer does not just change situations; it transforms the one who prays.

To truly understand the power of prayer, one must spend time in The Secret Place. God responds to the depth of your heart, not the length of your words. He listens to the cry of the sincere and responds to the faith of the expectant.

When prayer becomes your first response, not your last resort, you position yourself for victory. Prayer invites God to move where human effort fails. **Ask yourself:**

- Do I view prayer as a duty or as a divine privilege?
  - How can I cultivate a lifestyle of continual communion with God?
  - What areas of my life need to be surrendered in prayer today?

Divine Connection

Prayer is heaven's open line to the heart of God. It is more than a religious discipline; it is relationship in action. Through prayer, we are granted access to divine wisdom, guidance, and strength. When you pray, you enter a sacred exchange where your weakness meets His power, and your questions are met with His peace.

God never intended for prayer to be a ritual; He designed it to be relational. It is where you learn His voice, discern His will, and align your heart with His purpose. In prayer, God does not just change your circumstances; He transforms you.

Heaven's Authority Released

When you pray in faith, you are exercising spiritual authority. Prayer invites God's will to be done on earth as it is in heaven. Every victory in the visible world begins in the invisible realm of prayer. The walls of Jericho did not fall because of human strength; they fell because a people obeyed God and prayed with power.

Prayer is what transforms ordinary men and women into instruments of divine influence. Elijah prayed and the heavens shut. Daniel prayed and angels were dispatched. Jesus prayed and the dead were raised.

When you neglect prayer, you surrender your greatest weapon. But when you make prayer your priority, you invite heaven to fight on your behalf.

Transformation Through Prayer

Prayer molds your heart to reflect God's character. It strips away pride, self-reliance, and fear, and fills you with the fruit of the Spirit.

When you spend time with God, your speech changes, your thoughts are purified, and your spirit becomes sensitive to His leading. The power of prayer is not in eloquence, but in earnestness. God responds to hearts that are humble, sincere, and full of faith.

Consistency Builds Power

The strength of your prayer life is found in your consistency. Occasional prayer births moments, but consistent prayer births movements.

Make prayer a habit, not an emergency. When prayer becomes your lifestyle, the supernatural becomes natural.

Living in *The Secret Place*

The Secret Place is not a physical room; it is a posture of the heart. It is where your spirit dwells in constant awareness of God's presence. In this place, prayer is not an event, but an atmosphere. It is where you walk and talk with God daily, not just when you need something.

Those who live from *The Secret Place* carry peace in chaos, wisdom in confusion, and authority in adversity. Prayer is their oxygen. It sustains their soul and strengthens their spirit. But before prayer can operate in its full power, the heart must first be aligned.

A Prayer of Commitment

Father, I commit myself to prayer. Communion with You is not optional. Establish discipline and consistency in me. Teach me to seek You before I seek solutions. Order my priorities so that Your presence remains my foundation.

Let prayer govern my decisions, guard my heart, and align my life with Your will. I choose the Secret Place as my dwelling place. I will respond to Your instruction. In Jesus' name, Amen.

CHAPTER 2
True Repentance

For godly sorrow produces repentance leading to salvation, not to be regretted; but the sorrow of the world produces death.
2 Corinthians 7:10 NKJV

The Call to Return

Repentance is one of the greatest acts of love between God and His people. It is an open invitation to return to His presence and realign with His purpose. God's desire is not to condemn us, but to restore us. He longs for fellowship, and repentance is the pathway back into His embrace.

To repent means to change one's mind, to shift direction and turn away from sin. It is not just sorrow for what was done wrong. It is a decision to pursue what is right. Repentance is not weakness. It is wisdom. It is recognizing that life outside of God's will leads to emptiness, but life in His presence brings fulfillment and peace.

When we truly repent, we are not running from God. We are running to Him.

Conviction Versus Condemnation

There is a difference between conviction and condemnation.

- Condemnation pushes you away from God with guilt and shame.
- Conviction pulls you toward God with love and grace.

The enemy condemns to keep you bound. The Holy Spirit convicts to set you free. God does not remind you of your past to punish you. He reveals your heart so He can purify it.

The moment you respond to conviction with humility, grace meets you there. Forgiveness flows instantly, and your soul begins to heal.

The Broken and Contrite Heart

The sacrifices of God are a broken spirit, A broken and a contrite heart — These, O God, You will not despise.
Psalm 51:17 NKJV

David understood that true repentance was not about offering words or rituals. It was about offering the heart. His sin had separated him from the presence of God, and his cry for mercy came from deep within.

A contrite heart is one that admits, *"I cannot cleanse myself."* It recognizes that no amount of human effort can erase sin. Only the blood of Jesus can. God delights in honest surrender. When we come broken, He does not reject us. He rebuilds us.

Repentance is not about shame. It is about transformation.

Repentance Restores Fellowship

Sin separates, but repentance reconnects. It rebuilds the bridge between Creator and creation. Many people pray for revival, but revival cannot come without repentance. Every move of God begins with people humbling themselves, confessing their sins, and returning to holiness.

When the heart is cleansed, the heavens open. When the soul is surrendered, the Spirit flows freely.

Repentance restores fellowship, not just forgiveness. God does not only want to pardon you. He wants to walk with you again.

Turning, Not Just Talking

True repentance is more than verbal confession. It is visible transformation.

Confession says, *"Lord, I was wrong."* Repentance says, *"Lord, I will not go that way again."*

Words without change are empty. God looks beyond what we say and observes how we live. Repentance is confirmed in obedience.

When your heart is truly changed, your actions will follow. Your desires begin to shift. Your habits begin to break. Your focus begins to return to God's will. The change is not forced. It flows from a renewed spirit.

The Fruit of Repentance

Repentance always produces fruit, tangible evidence that your heart has been transformed.

- **Humility**: Pride is replaced with surrender.
- **Renewal**: The mind and spirit are refreshed by God's Word.
- **Obedience**: The will of God becomes your desire.
- **Peace**: Guilt is lifted, and inner rest is restored.
- **Power**: Purity revives your authority in prayer and ministry.

When repentance is genuine, others will notice the change. Your life becomes a testimony of grace, and your walk becomes a reflection of redemption.

Repentance Leads to Revival

Before God revives a nation, He revives the hearts of His people. The power of repentance is that it does not just transform individuals. It transforms families, churches, and communities.

When people return to God with sincere hearts, the atmosphere shifts. Healing comes. Joy returns.

The fire of His presence burns again. Repentance is the spark that ignites revival.

Repent therefore, and be converted, that your sins may be blotted out, so that times of refreshing may come from the presence of the Lord.
Acts 3:19 NKJV

Living a Lifestyle of Repentance

True repentance is not a one-time event. It is a lifestyle. Every day, the believer must allow the Holy Spirit to search the heart and reveal anything that does not honor God.

A repentant lifestyle keeps you spiritually sensitive, humble, and ready to receive divine instruction. It allows you to grow continually, unafraid of correction, and thankful for God's grace.

The closer you get to God, the more you desire to stay clean before Him. Repentance becomes less about guilt and more about relationship. It becomes your way of maintaining intimacy with a holy God.

A Prayer of Repentance

Father, I humble myself before You. Expose anything in my life that resists Your will. I confess without excuse and turn from every pattern that dishonors You.

Cleanse my heart. Renew my spirit. Restore fellowship and establish obedience within me. Repentance will not be an event. It will be my lifestyle.

I submit to Your correction and Your authority.

In Jesus' name, Amen.

CHAPTER 3
Changed Behavior

Therefore bear fruits worthy of repentance,
Matthew 3:8 NKJV

The Evidence of a Transformed Heart

True repentance always produces visible change. When the heart is genuinely touched by God, behavior follows. Words may express remorse, but behavior reveals transformation. Real repentance is not proven by emotion. It is proven by action.

When God cleanses the heart, the outer life must begin to reflect that inner work. The fruit of repentance is changed behavior. The same hands that once caused harm now help others. The same mouth that once gossiped now encourages. The same heart that once rebelled now seeks to obey.

A changed life is the loudest testimony of grace.

Change Begins Within

Transformation does not start in habits. It starts in the heart. God does not just modify behavior. He renews the mind and reshapes the spirit.

Do not be conformed to this world, but be transformed by the renewing of your mind…
Romans 12:2 NKJV

Until your mind changes, your behavior will always return to what it believes. That is why repentance is not just turning away from sin. It is turning toward truth. The more you fill your heart and mind with God's Word, the more your actions will align with His will.

Change produced by human effort fades. Change birthed by the Spirit remains.

The Proof of Surrender

Obedience is the truest form of worship. A surrendered heart no longer lives to please self but lives to please God. The mark of genuine repentance is a consistent desire to obey, even when it costs you comfort, convenience, or pride.

Change does not mean perfection. It means progress. Every day you choose to align with God's will is evidence that His Spirit is working within you.

For it is God who works in you both to will and to do for His good pleasure.
Philippians 2:13 NKJV

When you yield, He builds. When you surrender, He strengthens. When you obey, He establishes.

From Moment to Movement

Many experience moments of conviction but never allow those moments to become movements of transformation. God does not call us to temporary change. He calls us to lasting transformation.

True repentance brings a lifestyle shift, not a momentary pause. When your heart is changed, your appetite changes. What once attracted you now repels you. What once entertained you now burdens you. What once satisfied you now grieves your spirit.

That is the power of grace. It does not just forgive sin. It frees you from its control.

Signs of Changed Behavior

- **Consistency in Character:** You begin to live with integrity, whether seen or unseen.
- **Renewed Speech:** Your words start to reflect grace, gratitude, and truth.
- **Maturity in Reactions:** You respond with patience instead of anger, peace instead of panic.
- **Discipline in Decisions:** You think before acting, seeking God's guidance in every choice.
- **Compassion for Others:** The heart that was once hardened becomes tender toward others' needs.

Changed behavior does not happen overnight, but it does happen over time through consistent surrender. Each step of obedience becomes a testimony of God's transforming power.

The Role of Accountability

Sustained change thrives in the presence of accountability. God often uses spiritual leaders, mentors, and community to strengthen your walk. The enemy isolates. God connects. Surround yourself with those who challenge your growth and celebrate your obedience.

Change is not maintained in isolation but in relationship, with God and with godly counsel.

As iron sharpens iron, So a man sharpens the countenance of his friend.
Proverbs 27:17 NKJV

Grace for Growth

God does not expect perfection, but He does expect pursuit. Every believer walking in change will stumble at times, but grace picks us up, dusts us off, and pushes us forward.

Do not allow past failures to convince you that change is impossible. Every time you choose to get up and try again, Heaven rejoices. Growth is gradual, but it is necessary.

Change is not about trying harder. It is about trusting deeper. The Holy Spirit empowers what your flesh cannot accomplish.

True transformation is not sustained by emotion alone. A changed heart must be supported by a strong spiritual foundation. It is not enough to experience repentance and display its fruit; that change must be rooted in something that cannot be shaken.

Without a solid foundation in prayer, even genuine transformation can weaken over time. What God restores, He also desires to establish. That establishment begins with foundation.

CHAPTER 4
The Foundation of Prayer

Unless the Lord builds the house, They labor in vain who build it; Unless the Lord guards the city, The watchman stays awake in vain.
Psalm 127:1 NKJV

Prayer: The Cornerstone of Relationship

Every structure needs a foundation, and in the life of a believer, that foundation is prayer. Without it, faith weakens, purpose blurs, and strength fades. Prayer establishes spiritual stability. It is the unseen support beneath every victory, and every breakthrough.

Prayer is not an accessory to the Christian life; it is the anchor of it. It is where intimacy with God begins and where destiny is built. Without a foundation of prayer, the believer's life becomes like a house without a base, unstable, vulnerable, and easily shaken.

Built on Relationship, Not Religion

The foundation of prayer must be relationship, not religion. Prayer was never meant to be a ritual recited from obligation; it is meant to be a relationship cultivated from love.

When you pray out of duty, your words are empty. But when you pray out of desire, your spirit comes alive. True prayer flows from intimacy with God, knowing who He is, trusting His character, and believing His promises.

God is not impressed by how long you pray but by how real you are in your prayer. The foundation of prayer is honesty before God.

The Lord is near to all who call upon Him, To all who call upon Him in truth.
Psalm 145:18 NKJV

The Foundation of Faith

At its core, prayer is built on faith. Without faith, prayer becomes mere words; but with faith, those words become weapons. Faith turns prayer into power.

When you pray, you must believe that God not only hears but also responds. Faith gives prayer its authority. It reminds us that we are not speaking to a distant deity but to a loving Father who delights to answer His children.

And whatever you ask in prayer, believing, you will receive.
Matthew 21:22 NKJV

Faith is the foundation beneath every prayer that moves Heaven.

The Foundation of the Word

God responds to His Word. A strong prayer life is always rooted in Scripture. When you pray the Word of God, you are praying His will, and His will cannot fail.

Jesus used the Word to pray and to resist temptation. Every declaration, every victory, every breakthrough in prayer flows from knowing what God has already said. The Bible is your blueprint for effective prayer.

Pray the Word, speak the Word, and stand on the Word, because the Word is the foundation of faith filled prayer.

Then the Lord said to me, "You have seen well, for I am ready to perform My word."
Jeremiah 1:12 NKJV

The Foundation of Humility

A solid prayer foundation is built on humility. Prayer is not about proving how strong we are, it's about admitting how dependent we are. The posture of prayer is the posture of surrender.

Pride blocks prayer; humility invites God's presence. When we come before Him with open hearts and bowed spirits, Heaven leans in to listen.

But He gives more grace. Therefore He says: "God resists the proud, But gives grace to the humble."
James 4:6 NKJV

Humility reminds us that prayer is not manipulation, it's submission. We don't pray to control God's will; we pray to conform to it.

The Foundation of Consistency

The most powerful prayers are not always loud, long, or eloquent, they are consistent. Prayer builds momentum through discipline. Every time you pray, you're laying another brick in your spiritual foundation.

Consistency is what turns moments of prayer into a lifestyle of power. When you build your life on prayer, storms may come, but they cannot destroy what's rooted in God.

The Foundation of Surrender

At the deepest level, prayer is not about asking, it's about aligning. The strongest foundation of prayer is the one that says, "Not my will, but Yours be done."

True prayer is birthed in surrender. It's the moment you yield your plans for His purpose, your will for His wisdom, your timing for His truth. When your prayers become a reflection of His desires, answers flow without striving.

Surrender doesn't weaken your prayer life. It empowers it.

Building on the Rock

Jesus taught,

Therefore whoever hears these sayings of Mine, and does them, I will liken him to a wise man who built his house on the rock:

Matthew 7:24 NKJV

The rock is Christ Himself, the unshakable foundation of prayer. When your prayer life is built on Him, you cannot fall. Trials may come, seasons may shift, but your faith remains firm because your foundation is sure. A strong foundation prepares you to meet the conditions God attaches to answered prayer.

CHAPTER 5
The IF Factor

---

*IF My people, which are called by My name, shall humble themselves, and pray, and seek My face, and turn from their wicked ways; **THEN** will I heal their land.*

2 Chronicles 7:14 KJV

The Power of Divine Conditions

God, and throughout Scripture, His promises are often connected to divine conditions. The word "IF" is small in size but massive in significance. It reveals that while God is faithful, many of His promises are activated through our obedience.

The IF Factor teaches us that Heaven's response is often tied to Earth's responsibility. God is willing, ready, and able, but He is also just and intentional. The "IF" reveals our part in partnering with God for supernatural results.

The promise is guaranteed. Manifestation is conditional.

Responsibility Before Results

God does not withhold blessings out of cruelty; He withholds them out of order. He is teaching His people how to live in alignment with His will. The IF Factor is not about earning God's love, it's about positioning yourself to receive what He has already promised.

Many believers want the **THEN** without fulfilling the **IF**.

They want healing without humility.

They want breakthrough without prayer.

They want restoration without repentance.

But God's kingdom operates on divine order. Obedience unlocks access.

Breaking Down the IF

God gives us a clear pathway in *2 Chronicles 7:14:*

IF My people humble themselves

Humility acknowledges dependence on God. Pride blocks heaven. Humility invites grace.

IF they pray

Prayer is the communication of surrender. It shows God that you trust Him more than your own ability.

IF they seek My face

Seeking God's face means desiring His presence more than His hand. It is intimacy, not just intervention.

IF they turn from their wicked ways

This is repentance in action. It is changed direction, changed desire, and changed behavior.

Each condition builds upon the previous one. God's order cannot be bypassed without consequence.

From IF to THEN

God's response is clearly stated:

THEN will I hear from heaven.

THEN will I forgive their sin.

THEN will I heal their land.

Hearing.

Forgiving.

Healing.

These outcomes are divine responses to obedient alignment. The **IF** Factor positions God's people to experience the power of His **THEN.**

When God's conditions are met, His promises are released.

The IF Factor and Personal Breakthrough

Although this passage addresses a nation, the principle applies personally. Healing, restoration, clarity, and deliverance are often connected to our response to God's instruction.

Many prayers remain unanswered not because God is distant, but because alignment is lacking. The **IF** Factor is God's call to realignment so Heaven can respond without obstruction.

When humility, prayer, pursuit, and repentance are practiced, spiritual resistance is removed and divine flow is restored.

Faith That Acts

The IF Factor teaches us that faith is not passive. It is active. Real faith obeys. Real faith responds. Real faith aligns.

Thus also faith by itself, if it does not have works, is dead.
James 2:17 NKJV

The IF is your faith in action. It is your agreement with God's Word through obedience. When you move, God moves. When you align, God assigns. When you respond, God releases.

Delayed Blessings and the IF Factor

Sometimes what feels like delay is actually divine instruction. od waits for heart alignment before releasing what you are not prepared to steward.

The IF Factor is God's mercy. It prepares you for what you are praying for. It matures you before it manifests through you.

God will not release what you are not yet aligned to steward.

Living a Life of IF

The mature believer does not only pray for results. He lives in obedience daily. The IF Factor becomes a lifestyle, not a moment.

Every decision becomes a prayer. Every act of obedience becomes a key. Every step of humility becomes an invitation for Heaven to respond.

When IF becomes your lifestyle, THEN becomes your testimony.

A Prayer of Alignment and Obedience

Father, I humble myself before You. I will pray. I will seek Your face. I turn from every way that resists Your instruction.

Remove pride, delay, and compromise. Align my heart with Your requirements so Your promises are released without obstruction. Establish obedience within me. Position me for Your response. I choose alignment over convenience. In Jesus' name, Amen.

ALIGNMENT IN ACTION

Identify one area where humility, repentance, or obedience is required.

Address it without delay.

Remove any compromise that hinders alignment.

Establish consistent time in prayer.

Reorder your priorities to reflect pursuit of God.

Where alignment is restored, manifestation follows.

CHAPTER 6
The Key to a Maximized Prayer Life

Pray without ceasing.
1 Thessalonians 5:17 KJV

A maximized prayer life is not built on routine alone. It is built on relationship. Routine may help you begin, but relationship keeps you connected. The key to maximizing your prayer life is shifting from obligation to desire.

When prayer becomes your first love instead of your last resort, your spiritual life changes. You no longer pray only because you need something. You pray because you need Him.

Prayer flows from intimacy, not just information.

Consistency Is the Master Key

Consistency is one of the greatest keys to spiritual growth. Occasional prayer produces occasional results, but consistent prayer produces lasting strength.

Jesus often withdrew to lonely places to pray. Daniel prayed three times a day. The early church continued steadfastly in prayer. Their power did not come from one powerful moment, but from a faithful pattern.

Consistency turns prayer into a lifestyle. It trains your spirit to remain sensitive to God and attentive to His voice.

Hunger and Desire

Spiritual hunger unlocks deeper levels of prayer. God responds to those who truly desire Him. A satisfied believer rarely prays deeply, but a hungry believer seeks God with urgency.

Blessed are those who hunger and thirst for righteousness, for they shall be filled.
Matthew 5:6 NKJV

Hunger produces pursuit. Pursuit produces intimacy. Intimacy releases power.

Prayer Fueled by the Word

The Word of God gives prayer direction and authority. When you pray Scripture, you are praying in alignment with God's will. The Word strengthens faith, sharpens focus, and anchors what you declare.

Without the Word, prayer drifts into emotion. Grounded in the Word, it becomes steady and effective. When the Word is in your mouth and faith is in your heart, your prayers move from simple requests to confident declarations.

Sensitivity to the Holy Spirit

A maximized prayer life is led by the Spirit. The Holy Spirit teaches you what to pray, how to pray, and when to pray. Sometimes prayer is spoken aloud. Sometimes it is silent. Sometimes it is waiting. Sometimes it is spiritual warfare.

Those who are sensitive to the Spirit learn to follow His promptings. He may lead you to intercede, to worship, to repent, or simply to be still. Each posture has purpose.

Likewise the Spirit also helps in our weaknesses.

For we do not know what we should pray for as we ought, but the Spirit Himself makes intercession for us with groanings which cannot be uttered.
Romans 8:26 NKJV

Prayer and Obedience

Obedience strengthens prayer. Disobedience weakens spiritual flow. When your life aligns with God's will, your prayers carry greater confidence. When you walk uprightly, you pray with assurance. When your heart is clean, your voice is steady.

Confess your trespasses to one another, and pray for one another, that you may be healed. The effective, fervent prayer of a righteous man avails much.
James 5:16 NKJV

Righteous living supports righteous praying.

Eliminating Distractions

Another key to maximizing prayer is guarding your focus. A distracted spirit struggles to pray deeply. The enemy does not always try to stop prayer. Sometimes he weakens it through distraction.

Intentional time set apart from noise and interruption allows your spirit to go deeper. *The Secret Place* requires separation before it produces revelation. Depth requires discipline.

Faith That Expects

Expectation prepares the way for answered prayer. When you pray believing, you pray with confidence. Doubt weakens faith, but trust strengthens it.

Those who believe God will move pray with assurance and persistence. They pray knowing that Heaven hears.

The Lifestyle of Prayer

Prayer is not limited to a prayer closet. It becomes a way of living. You pray while driving. You pray while working. You pray while waiting. You remain in communion with God throughout the day.

Prayer becomes breathing. Worship becomes natural. Fellowship becomes continual. This is a life of spiritual maturity. When a prayer life is strengthened and sustained, results naturally follow.

A Prayer of Consistency

Father, strengthen my discipline in prayer. Remove every distraction that weakens my focus. Increase my hunger for Your presence and sharpen my spiritual sensitivity.

Teach me to guard time with You above competing demands. Establish consistency that produces endurance and strength. My prayer life will not be occasional. It will be sustained. I commit to private devotion and disciplined pursuit. In Jesus' name, Amen.

CHAPTER 7
Pray to Get Results

Ye lust, and have not: ye kill, and desire to have, and cannot obtain: ye fight and war, yet ye have not, because ye ask not.
James 4:2 KJV

Prayer That Produces

God never intended prayer to be empty words or religious routine. Prayer was designed to produce results. When you pray according to God's will, in faith and in alignment, you can trust that God hears. Results are not accidental. They are intentional.

Prayer is not simply spiritual activity. It is spiritual authority in action. Prayer aligns the believer with what God desires to accomplish.

When prayer is aligned, results follow.

Asking with Boldness

Many believers pray timidly, but Scripture teaches us to pray with boldness. God is not intimidated by faith. He invites us to come boldly before His throne.

Let us therefore come boldly unto the throne of grace, that we may obtain mercy, and find grace to help in time of need.
Hebrews 4:16 KJV

Bold prayer is not arrogance. It is confidence in God's character. When you know who God is, you pray with expectation. You do not rely on chance. You trust His nature.

Faith That Activates Heaven

Faith is essential in prayer. Prayer without faith becomes routine. Prayer with faith becomes effective.

But without faith it is impossible to please him: for he that cometh to God must believe that he is, and that he is a rewarder of them that diligently seek him.
Hebrews 11:6 KJV

When you pray believing, you position yourself to receive. Faith is not denial of reality. It is confidence in God's ability to intervene.

Praying with Persistence

Some answers require persistence. Jesus taught that men ought always to pray and not faint. Delay does not mean denial. Persistence reveals faith.

The persistent widow received justice because she did not give up. Elijah prayed seven times before the rain came. Persistence keeps the believer faithful while waiting on God's response.

If you stop praying, you remove yourself from the process. Persistence strengthens your expectation.

Praying According to God's Will

Results are connected to alignment with God's will. God confirms what He has already spoken.

The closer your prayers reflect His Word, the greater your confidence in the outcome.

And this is the confidence that we have in him, that, if we ask any thing according to his will, he heareth us:
1 John 5:14 KJV

When you pray the Word of God, you remove uncertainty. You stand on what He has already declared.

Removing Spiritual Hindrances

Unforgiveness, disobedience, and hidden sin can hinder the effectiveness of prayer. God hears, but alignment matters.

Jesus taught that unforgiveness affects prayer. Repentance and obedience restore clarity and remove obstacles. Clean hands and a pure heart create spiritual clarity.

Speaking with Authority

Prayer includes both asking and declaring. When you understand your authority in Christ, your prayers reflect that understanding.

Death and life are in the power of the tongue: And they that love it shall eat the fruit thereof.
Proverbs 18:21 KJV

Speak in agreement with God's Word. Your words, when aligned with faith and Scripture, carry weight.

Expecting Manifestation

Expectation reflects faith. Those who expect results prepare for them. Expectation keeps your heart attentive to what God is doing.

If you pray for open doors, watch for opportunity.

If you pray for healing, look for progress.

If you pray for provision, remain attentive to supply.

Faith prepares before the answer is visible.

From Prayer to Praise

Praise demonstrates trust. Praising God before the answer appears demonstrates confidence in Him. Paul and Silas prayed, and they praised. Their praise preceded their release. Praise confirms that you believe God is working.

A Lifestyle of Results

Results do not come from occasional intense prayer. They come from consistent, aligned living. When prayer becomes your practice, results become evident.

Your life becomes testimony.

Your breakthroughs strengthen others.

Your faith encourages those who are still waiting.

A Prayer for Bold and Effective Faith

Father, I come before You in faith and expectation. I align my requests with Your Word and Your will. Remove doubt. Strengthen confidence in Your promises.

Teach me persistence without wavering. I will not pray timidly. I will pray with boldness and authority. Let my prayer life produce results that glorify You and advance Your purpose.

In Jesus' name, Amen.

CHAPTER 8
Talking to God

Call unto me, and I will answer thee, and shew thee great and mighty things, which thou knowest not.
Jeremiah 33:3 KJV

Prayer as Conversation

Talking to God is the heart of prayer. It is not a speech. It is a conversation. God never intended prayer to be one sided. He desires dialogue, not monologue. When you talk to God, you open your heart to the One who knows you completely and loves you unconditionally.

Prayer gains power when it becomes personal. You do not need perfect words. You need an honest heart. God is more concerned with sincerity than vocabulary. He listens for truth, not performance. When you learn to talk to God, prayer becomes natural instead of forced.

God Desires Your Voice

God is not distant. He is a Father who desires to hear from His children. Just as an earthly father delights in hearing the voice of his child, your heavenly Father delights in hearing your voice in prayer.

Every concern matters to Him. Every tear is seen. Every whisper is heard. Talking to God invites Him into the details of your life, not only the major decisions but the daily moments as well.

When you talk to God, you acknowledge your dependence and welcome His involvement.

Come As You Are

One of the greatest misunderstandings about prayer is the belief that you must be perfect to pray. God invites you to come as you are, whether broken, tired, confused, or joyful. Prayer is not about pretending. It is about presenting your true self before a holy God who heals and restores.

Honest prayer opens the door for real healing. God heals what you are willing to reveal. When you talk to God from a place of truth, He responds with grace.

Bringing Your Whole Heart

God does not only invite you to come as you are. He invites you to come completely. Prayer is not limited to composed words and controlled emotions. It is the place where you bring what is real before Him.

There will be seasons of confidence and seasons of questions. Seasons of clarity and seasons of uncertainty. God is not distant in those moments. He remains present. Honest prayer does not weaken faith. It strengthens relationship.

When parts of the heart are withheld, intimacy is limited. The Secret Place is not designed for performance. It is designed for communion. Transparency deepens trust. Sincerity strengthens connection.

Bring your concerns. Bring your gratitude. Bring your need for direction. When you bring your whole heart before God, you position yourself for deeper fellowship and greater peace.

Listening Is Part of Talking

Talking to God also includes learning to listen. Prayer is not complete until you make room for His voice. Sometimes God speaks through His Word. Sometimes He speaks through His Spirit. Sometimes He confirms direction through peace or conviction.

Stillness creates space for clarity. When you quiet your heart, you become more attentive to His direction. Listening brings guidance to prayer.

Sharing Your Heart with God

God invites you to share everything, your fears, frustrations, hopes, dreams, and desires. Nothing is too small and nothing is too great for Him. Talking to God brings release as you lay down what weighs you down and receive His peace. In His presence, burdens are lifted and hearts are strengthened.

Talking to God Throughout the Day

Prayer is not confined to a specific place. You can talk to God while driving, working, resting, or walking. Continual conversation builds awareness of His presence.

When you develop the habit of speaking with God throughout the day, your relationship deepens. He becomes more than someone you visit. He becomes someone you walk with.

From Talking to Trusting

The more you talk to God, the more you trust Him. Communication builds confidence. As you share your heart, you grow in the assurance that He cares for you.

Talking to God strengthens faith and settles anxiety. It reminds you that you are never alone and never unheard.

Talking to God in Difficult Seasons

In painful seasons, talking to God becomes essential. When people fail you, God remains faithful. When answers are delayed, God is still present. Talking to God keeps your heart steady when life feels uncertain. Honesty in hardship becomes a pathway to healing.

CHAPTER 9
Listening to God

My sheep hear my voice, and I know them, and they follow me:
John 10:27 KJV

The Other Half of Prayer

Prayer is incomplete without listening. Talking to God builds relationship, but listening to God provides direction. God speaks through His Word, His Spirit, and His peace. The issue is not whether God is speaking, but whether we are positioned to hear Him.

Listening turns prayer from expression into instruction. It shifts prayer from emotional release to spiritual guidance. When you listen, you move from pouring out to receiving.

Creating Space to Hear

Hearing God requires intentional stillness. In a loud world, quiet becomes sacred. You cannot hear clearly if your heart remains distracted.

God often speaks in a still, small voice. Silence is not empty. It is an invitation. When you quiet your spirit, you create room for divine communication. Stillness is spiritual positioning.

God Speaks Through His Word

The primary way God speaks is through Scripture. His Word is His voice in written form. When you read the Bible, you are not simply reading history. You are receiving truth, correction, encouragement, and direction.

If you want to hear God clearly, spend time in His Word daily. The more familiar you become with Scripture, the easier it is to recognize His voice. God will never speak in a way that contradicts His Word.

The Voice of the Holy Spirit

The Holy Spirit is your guide. He speaks through conviction, peace, inner promptings, and spiritual impressions. He leads, warns, comforts, and directs.

Sometimes His voice comes as a gentle nudge. Sometimes as a check in your spirit. Sometimes as a deep sense of peace or unrest. Learning to listen requires sensitivity and obedience. The more you respond to His leading, the clearer His voice becomes.

Discerning God's Voice

Discerning God's voice requires maturity and consistency. His voice brings peace, clarity, and alignment with His Word.

Confusion, fear, and condemnation do not come from God. His voice corrects without crushing. It convicts and it comforts. As you grow, you learn to distinguish between God's voice, your own thoughts, and the enemy's lies.

Obedience Sharpens Hearing

Hearing is strengthened by obedience. When you respond to what God says, He entrusts you with greater clarity. Disobedience dulls spiritual awareness, but obedience refines it.

Spiritual maturity is not measured only by how clearly you hear God's voice. It is revealed in how faithfully you act on what He says. Hearing without response weakens sensitivity. Obedience strengthens discernment.

As you grow, you will recognize that God often speaks with direction that requires movement. He may prompt you to adjust your attitude, correct your approach, forgive quickly, or step forward in faith. These instructions are not burdens. They are opportunities for growth. Every act of obedience builds stability in your walk with Him.

When you respond consistently, your confidence increases. Direction becomes clearer. Peace becomes steadier. Obedience does not restrict you. It advances you.

God speaks to those who are willing to follow. If you desire clearer direction, respond faithfully to the last instruction He gave you. Obedience keeps your spiritual hearing active and your life aligned.

Listening in Difficult Seasons

In difficult seasons, listening requires trust. There will be times when God does not immediately remove the storm. Instead, He strengthens you to walk through it.

When answers feel delayed or direction seems minimal, do not assume God is absent. Silence is not abandonment. At times, His quietness is an invitation to remain steady and anchored in what He has already spoken.

Difficult seasons test not only what you hear, but what you believe. Listening in hardship is less about receiving new instruction and more about holding firmly to established truth. When circumstances shift, God's character does not.

In seasons of uncertainty, trust becomes your anchor. You may not always receive detailed explanations, but you will receive peace to endure. As you remain attentive to His presence, endurance is formed and faith is strengthened.

Listening in the valley prepares you for stability on the mountain. Trust sustained over time deepens intimacy and strengthens confidence in God's faithfulness.

Journaling and Spiritual Awareness

Writing down what you hear God saying strengthens clarity and builds confidence. Journaling allows you to reflect, recognize patterns, and trace how God has led you over time. What feels unclear in the moment often becomes evident when you look back.

Recording what you hear also helps you measure it against Scripture and wise counsel. God does not contradict His Word. He confirms His direction through peace and alignment.

Spiritual awareness grows through reflection. As you review how God has guided you, your confidence in His voice becomes stronger. Those who learn to hear God clearly walk with steady assurance. Following His voice positions them under His protection and prepares them to live securely under His covering.

CHAPTER 10
Covered to Recover

And I will restore to you the years that the locust hath eaten, the cankerworm, and the caterpillar, and the palmerworm, my great army which I sent among you.
Joel 2:25 KJV

The Power of Divine Covering

God restores what He first covers. Divine covering is His protection, presence, and provision surrounding your life. When you are covered by God, you are sustained in adversity and positioned for recovery.

To be covered means you are placed under His authority and care. Under His covering, what was meant to destroy you becomes a testimony of His faithfulness.

Covering is protection, and it is preparation for recovery.

From Exposure to Protection

Many are wounded because they were spiritually exposed through prayerlessness, disobedience, or isolation. Yet God's grace provides a way back into divine covering. Through repentance, prayer, and obedience, you return to His shelter.

He that dwelleth in the secret place of the Most High Shall abide under the shadow of the Almighty.
Psalm 91:1 KJV

The Secret Place is a place of covering. When you live under His shadow, you are hidden from what was sent to harm you. Exposure creates vulnerability. Covering provides security.

Covered to Recover What Was Lost

God's promise is not only protection but restoration. Recovery is His response to obedience and alignment. What was lost in seasons of warfare, poor decisions, betrayal, or delay is not beyond His reach.

When God covers you, He positions you to recover what was taken. Peace, joy, relationships, and purpose are not beyond His reach.

Recovery is not wishful thinking. It is covenant promise.

The Role of Grace in Recovery

Grace is God's provision for recovery. You do not recover because you deserve it. You recover because God is merciful. Grace not only forgives your past but strengthens your future.

Grace covers weakness while God strengthens obedience. Under grace, shame is removed and hope is restored. God covers mistakes so He can recover destiny. Grace does not excuse disobedience. It empowers transformation.

Healing Under the Covering

Many struggle to recover because they have not allowed God to heal what was broken. Healing is part of recovery. God restores not only circumstances but people.

Under His covering, emotional wounds, spiritual scars, and hidden pain are brought into His healing presence. He heals so you can move forward without carrying unresolved hurt into your future.

Covered hearts become healed hearts. Healed hearts become restored lives.

Restoration Requires Positioning

Recovery requires positioning. You must remain under God's covering to experience sustained restoration. As a roof protects a house, spiritual covering protects your progress.

Remaining connected to prayer, the Word, and godly counsel keeps you steady. What God restores must be guarded. What He rebuilds must be maintained. Where God covers, the enemy cannot control.

From Survival to Restoration

God does not intend for you to merely survive. He intends for you to recover and thrive. What the enemy meant to end you, God uses to elevate you. Survival becomes a testimony. Recovery becomes evidence of His faithfulness.

You are not only coming out. You are coming back stronger. Covered to recover means you are protected while God rebuilds.

A Prayer for Restoration

Father, I position myself under Your covering. Restore what has been lost. Heal what has been damaged. Strengthen what was weakened by delay or disobedience.

I choose obedience, alignment, and accountability. Let Your covenant promise of restoration manifest in my life. Rebuild what warfare attempted to destroy. Establish me securely under Your authority. I will remain covered and aligned. In Jesus' name, Amen.

ALIGNMENT IN ACTION

Return to disciplined prayer and remain consistent in the Word.

Strengthen accountability in your spiritual walk.

Guard what God restores in your life.

Refuse patterns that created spiritual exposure.

Recovery is sustained when you remain covered and aligned.

STRUCTURED PRAYER PRACTICE

As you continue in the Secret Place, structure will support consistency. The following pattern offers a simple order to help maintain alignment in your daily prayer life.

1. **Pray the Word First**

   Begin with Scripture. Declare what God has spoken. When you pray the Word, you align your heart with His will and establish authority in your prayer.

2. **Humble Yourself**

   Approach God with sincerity and submission. Acknowledge your dependence on Him.

3. **Maintain a Repentant Heart**

   Confess anything that hinders clarity. Stay sensitive to conviction and responsive to correction.

4. **Present Your Requests**

   Ask specifically and in faith. Pray with confidence that God hears and responds.

5. **Listen Intentionally**

   Create space for His voice. Remain attentive to His direction.

6. **Close with Thanksgiving**

   End with gratitude. Thank Him for His presence, His guidance, and His faithfulness.

   Consistency transforms structure into lifestyle.

THE SEAL OF COMPLETION

This book began with prayer and ends with recovery. That reflects God's order. Prayer positions you. Repentance cleanses you. Changed behavior aligns you. Intimacy sustains you. Listening directs you. Covering restores you.

The Secret Place must now become your daily practice. It cannot remain an idea or a moment of inspiration. It must become your posture and your pursuit.

Remain under His covering. Guard what He restores. Continue in prayer. Do not drift from what brought you into alignment.

This is not merely information. It is instruction. Live it consistently, and you will remain positioned, protected, and restored in the presence of God.

ACKNOWLEDGEMENTS

I give honor and gratitude to my parents, Dr. Cecil Bridgeforth and Charlette Bridgeforth. My father's life remains a testimony of perseverance, faith, and the sustaining power of prayer. Even in seasons of intense health challenges, he demonstrated unwavering trust in God and confidence in divine healing. His example shaped my understanding of prayer not merely as a discipline, but as a lifeline.

My mother has modeled steadfast love, strength, and faithful support through every season. Her commitment, both in private intercession and visible endurance, has revealed the quiet power of standing in faith beside those you love.

To my wife, Madelene Bridgeforth, thank you for your unwavering support, your encouragement, and your consistent prayers. Your strength and spiritual covering have been instrumental in every season of this journey.

To my children and my church family, thank you for your love, your support, and your prayers. They do not go unnoticed. Your faithfulness and belief in the vision have helped carry this assignment forward.

This work stands as evidence of what God accomplishes through prayer, faith, and faithful relationships.

BISHOP
CECIL E. BRIDGEFORTH

888.794.7941

www.bishopbridgeforth.com

info@bishopbridgeforth.com

CONCISE
PUBLISHING HOUSE

This work was stewarded under the Concise Publishing House imprint, a curated house committed to bringing purpose-driven manuscripts to publication with clarity, integrity, and care.

Publishing & Production
Book Design & Formatting
ISBN & Distribution Guidance
Author Support

www.ConcisePublishing.us